The Lamplighter - A Farce In One Act by Charles Dickens

Charles Dickens (1812-1870) is regarded by many readers and literary critics to be THE major English novelist of the Victorian Age. He is remembered today as the author of a series of weighty novels which have been translated into many languages and promoted to the rank of World Classics. The latter include, but are not limited to, *The Adventures of Oliver Twist*, *A Tale of Two Cities*, *David Copperfield*, *A Christmas Carol*, *Hard Times*, *Great Expectations* and *The Old Curiosity Shop*.
His talents extended to many other forms including short stories, poetry, letters and his serial magazines. Of course being such a talent he also wrote plays. We are very pleased to present his fourth of four plays

Index Of Contents

DRAMATIS PERSONAE
MR. STARGAZER.
MASTER GALILEO ISAAC NEWTON FLAMSTEAD STARGAZER (his son).
TOM GRIG (the Lamplighter).
MR. MOONEY (an Astrologer).
SERVANT.
BETSY MARTIN.
EMMA STARGAZER.
FANNY BROWN.

THE LAMPLIGHTER

SCENE I.—The Street, outside of MR. STARGAZER'S house.
Two street Lamp-posts in front.

TOM GRIG (with ladder and lantern, singing as he enters).
Day has gone down o'er the Baltic's proud bil-ler;
Evening has sigh'd, alas! to the lone wil-ler;
Night hurries on, night hurries on, earth and ocean to kiv-ver;
Rise, gentle moon, rise, gentle moon, and guide me to my—

That ain't a rhyme, that ain't—kiv-ver and lover! I ain't much of a poet; but if I couldn't make better verse than that, I'd undertake to be set fire to, and put up, instead of the lamp, before Alderman Waithman's obstacle in Fleet-street. Bil-ler, wil-ler, kiv-ver—shiver, obviously. That's what I call poetry. (Sings.)

Day has gone down o'er the Baltic's proud bil-ler—

(During the previous speech he has been occupied in lighting one of the lamps. As he is about to light the other, MR. STARGAZER appears at window, with a telescope.)

MR. STARGAZER (after spying most intently at the clouds). Holloa!

TOM (on ladder). Sir, to you! And holloa again, if you come to that.

MR. STARGAZER. Have you seen the comet?

TOM. What Comet—The Exeter Comet?

MR. STARGAZER. What comet? The comet—Halley's comet!

TOM. Nelson's, you mean. I saw it coming out of the yard, not five minutes ago.

MR. STARGAZER. Could you distinguish anything of a tail?

TOM. Distinguish a tail? I believe you—four tails!

MR. STARGAZER. A comet with four tails; and all visible to the naked eye! Nonsense, it couldn't be.

TOM. You wouldn't say that again if you was down here, old Bantam. (Clock strikes five.) You'll tell me next, I suppose, that that isn't five o'clock striking, eh?

MR. STARGAZER. Five o'clock—five o'clock! Five o'clock P.M. on the thirtieth day of November, one thousand eight hundred and thirty-eight! Stop till I come down—stop! Don't go away on any account—not a foot, not a step. (Closes window.)

TOM (descending, and shouldering his ladder). Stop! stop, to a lamplighter, with three hundred and seventy shops and a hundred and twenty private houses waiting to be set a light to! Stop, to a lamplighter!

As he is running off, enter MR. STARGAZER from his house, hastily.

MR. STARGAZER (detaining him). Not for your life!—not for your life! The thirtieth day of November, one thousand eight hundred and thirty-eight! Miraculous circumstance! extraordinary fulfilment of a prediction of the planets!

TOM. What are you talking about?

MR. STARGAZER (looking about). Is there nobody else in sight, up the street or down? No, not a soul! This, then, is the man whose coming was revealed to me by the stars, six months ago!

TOM. What do you mean?

MR. STARGAZER. Young man, that I have consulted the Book of Fate with rare and wonderful success,—that coming events have cast their shadows before.

TOM. Don't talk nonsense to me,—I ain't an event; I'm a lamplighter!

MR. STARGAZER. (aside). True!—Strange destiny that one, announced by the planets as of noble birth, should be devoted to so humble an occupation. (Aloud.) But you were not always a lamplighter?

TOM. Why, no. I wasn't born with a ladder on my left shoulder, and a light in my other hand. But I took to it very early, though,—I had it from my uncle.

MR. STARGAZER (aside). He had it from his uncle! How plain, and yet how forcible, is his language! He speaks of lamplighting, as though it were the whooping-cough or measles! (To him.) Ay!

TOM. Yes, he was the original. You should have known him!—'cod! he was a genius, if ever there was one. Gas was the death of him! When gas lamps was first talked of, my uncle draws himself up, and says, 'I'll not believe it, there's no sich a thing,' he says. 'You might as well talk of laying on an everlasting succession of glow-worms!' But when they made the experiment of lighting a piece of Pall Mall—

MR. STARGAZER. That was when it first came up?

TOM. No, no, that was when it was first laid down. Don't mind me; I can't help a joke, now and then. My uncle was sometimes took that way. When the experiment was made of lighting a piece of Pall Mall, and he had actually witnessed it, with his own eyes, you should have seen my uncle then!

MR. STARGAZER. So much overcome?

TOM. Overcome, sir! He fell off his ladder, from weakness, fourteen times that very night; and his last fall was into a wheelbarrow that was going his way, and humanely took him home. 'I foresee in this,' he says, 'the breaking up of our profession; no more polishing of the tin reflectors,' he says; 'no more fancy-work, in the way of clipping the cottons at two o'clock in the morning; no more going the rounds to trim by daylight, and dribbling down of the ile on the hats and bonnets of the ladies and gentlemen, when one feels in good spirits. Any low fellow can light a gas-lamp, and it's all up!' So he petitioned the government for—what do you call that that they give to people when it's found out that they've never been of any use, and have been paid too much for doing nothin?

MR. STARGAZER. Compensation?

TOM. Yes, that's the thing,—compensation. They didn't give him any, though! And then he got very fond of his country all at once, and went about, saying how that the bringing in of gas was a death-blow to his native land, and how that its ile and cotton trade was gone for ever, and the whales would go and kill themselves, privately, in spite and vexation at not being caught! After this, he was right-down cracked, and called his 'bacco pipe a gas pipe, and thought his tears was lamp ile, and all manner of nonsense. At last, he went and hung himself on a lamp iron, in St. Martin's Lane, that he'd always been very fond of; and as he was a remarkably good husband, and had never had any secrets from his wife, he put a note in the twopenny post, as he went along, to tell the widder where the body was.

MR. STARGAZER (laying his hand upon his arm, and speaking mysteriously). Do you remember your parents?

TOM. My mother I do, very well!

MR. STARGAZER. Was she of noble birth?

TOM. Pretty well. She was in the mangling line. Her mother came of a highly respectable family,—such a business, in the sweetstuff and hardbake way!

MR. STARGAZER. Perhaps your father was—

TOM. Why, I hardly know about him. The fact is, there was some little doubt, at the time, who was my father. Two or three young gentlemen were paid the pleasing compliment; but their incomes being limited, they were compelled delicately to decline it.

MR. STARGAZER. Then the prediction is not fulfilled merely in part, but entirely and completely. Listen, young man,—I am acquainted with all the celestial bodies—

TOM. Are you, though?—I hope they are quite well,—every body.

MR. STARGAZER. Don't interrupt me. I am versed in the great sciences of astronomy and astrology; in my house there I have every description of apparatus for observing the course and motion of the planets. I'm writing a work about them, which will consist of eighty-four volumes, imperial quarto; and an appendix, nearly twice as long. I read what's going to happen in the stars.

TOM. Read what's going to happen in the stars! Will anything particular happen in the stars in the course of next week, now?

MR. STARGAZER. You don't understand me. I read in the stars what's going to happen here. Six months ago I derived from this source the knowledge that, precisely as the clock struck five, on the afternoon of this very day, a stranger would present himself before my enraptured sight,—that stranger would be a man of illustrious and high descent,—that stranger would be the destined husband of my young and lovely niece, who is now beneath that roof (points to his house);—that stranger is yourself: I receive you with open arms!

TOM. Me! I, the man of illustrious and high—I, the husband of a young and lovely—Oh! it can't be, you know! the stars have made a mistake—the comet has put 'em out!

MR. STARGAZER. Impossible! The characters were as plain as pike-staves. The clock struck five; you were here; there was not a soul in sight; a mystery envelopes your birth; you are a man of noble aspect. Does not everything combine to prove the accuracy of my observations?

TOM. Upon my word, it looks like it! And now I come to think of it, I have very often felt as if I wasn't the small beer I was taken for. And yet I don't know,—you're quite sure about the noble aspect?

MR. STARGAZER. Positively certain.

TOM. Give me your hand.

MR. STARGAZER. And my heart, too! (They shake hands heartily.)

TOM. The young lady is tolerably good-looking, is she?

MR. STARGAZER. Beautiful! A graceful carriage, an exquisite shape, a sweet voice; a countenance beaming with animation and expression; the eye of a startled fawn.

TOM. I see; a sort of game eye. Does she happen to have any of the—this is quite between you and me, you know,—and I only ask from curiosity,—not because I care about it,—any of the ready?

MR. STARGAZER. Five thousand pounds! But what of that? what of that? A word in your ear. I'm in search of the philosopher's stone! I have very nearly found it—not quite. It turns everything to gold; that's its property.

TOM. What a lot of property it must have!

MR. STARGAZER. When I get it, we'll keep it in the family. Not a word to any one! What will money be to us? We shall never be able to spend it fast enough.

TOM. Well, you know, we can but try,—I'll do my best endeavours.

MR. STARGAZER. Thank you,—thank you! But I'll introduce you to your future bride at once:—this way, this way!

TOM. What, without going my rounds first?

MR. STARGAZER. Certainly. A man in whom the planets take especial interest, and who is about to have a share in the philosopher's stone, descend to lamplighting!

TOM. Perish the base idea! not by no means! I'll take in my tools, though, to prevent any kind inquiries after me, at your door. (As he shoulders the ladder the sound of violent rain is heard.) Holloa.

MR. STARGAZER (putting his hand on his head in amazement). What's that?

TOM. It's coming down, rather.

MR. STARGAZER. Rain!

TOM. Ah! and a soaker, too!

MR. STARGAZER. It can't be!—it's impossible!—(Taking a book from his pocket, and turning over the pages hurriedly.) Look here,—here it is,—here's the weather almanack,—'Set fair,'—I knew it couldn't be! (with great triumph).

TOM (turning up his collar as the rain increases). Don't you think there's a dampness in the atmosphere?

MR. STARGAZER (looking up). It's singular,—it's like rain!

TOM. Uncommonly like.

MR. STARGAZER. It's a mistake in the elements, somehow. Here it is, 'set fair,'—and set fair it ought to be. 'Light clouds floating about.' Ah! you see, there are no light clouds;—the weather's all wrong.

TOM. Don't you think we had better get under cover?

MR. STARGAZER (slowly retreating towards the house). I don't acknowledge that it has any right to rain, mind! I protest against this. If Nature goes on in this way, I shall lose all respect for her,—it won't do, you know; it ought to have been two degrees colder, yesterday; and instead of that, it was warmer. This is not the way to treat scientific men. I protest against it!

[Exeunt into house, both talking, TOM pushing STARGAZER on, and the latter continually turning back, to declaim against the weather.

SCENE II.—A room in STARGAZER'S house. BETSY MARTIN, EMMA STARGAZER, FANNY BROWN, and GALILEO, all murmuring together as they enter.

BETSY. I say, again, young ladies, that it's shameful! unbearable!

ALL. Oh! shameful! shameful!

BETSY. Marry Miss Emma to a great, old, ugly, doting, dreaming As-tron-o-Magician, like Mr. Mooney, who's always winking and blinking through telescopes and that, and can't see a pretty face when it's under his very nose!

GALILEO (with a melancholy air). There never was a pretty face under his nose, Betsy, leastways, since I've known him. He's very plain.

BETSY. Ah! there's poor young master, too; he hasn't even spirits enough to laugh at his own jokes. I'm sure I pity him, from the very bottom of my heart.

FANNY and EMMA. Poor fellow!

GALILEO. Ain't I a legitimate subject for pity? Ain't it a dreadful thing that I, that am twenty-one come next Lady-day, should be treated like a little boy?—and all because my father is so busy with the moon's age that he don't care about mine; and so much occupied in making observations on the sun round which the earth revolves, that he takes no notice of the son that revolves round him! I wasn't taken out of nankeen frocks and trousers till I became quite unpleasant in 'em.

ALL. What a shame!

GALILEO. I wasn't, indeed. And look at me now! Here's a state of things. Is this a suit of clothes for a major,—at least, for a gentleman who is a minor now, but will be a major on the very next Lady-day that comes? Is this a fit—

ALL (interrupting him). Certainly not!

GALILEO (vehemently). I won't stand it—I won't submit to it any longer. I will be married.

ALL. No, no, no! don't be rash.

GALILEO. I will, I tell you. I'll marry my cousin Fanny. Give me a kiss, Fanny; and Emma and Betsy will look the other way the while. (Kisses her.) There!

BETSY. Sir—sir! here's your father coming!

GALILEO. Well, then, I'll have another, as an antidote to my father. One more, Fanny. (Kisses her.)

MR. STARGAZER (without). This way! this way! You shall behold her immediately.

Enter MR. STARGAZER, TOM following bashfully.

MR. STARGAZER. Where is my—? Oh, here she is! Fanny, my dear, come here. Do you see that gentleman? (Aside.)

FANNY. What gentleman, uncle? Do you mean that elastic person yonder who is bowing with so much perseverance?

MR. STARGAZER. Hush! Yes; that's the interesting stranger.
FANNY. Why, he is kissing his hand, uncle. What does the creature mean?

MR. STARGAZER. Ah, the rogue! Just like me, before I married your poor aunt,—all fire and impatience. He means love, my darling, love. I've such a delightful surprise for you. I didn't tell you before, for fear there should be any mistake; but it's all right, it's all right. The stars have settled it all among 'em. He's to be your husband!

FANNY. My husband, uncle? Goodness gracious, Emma! (Converses apart with her.)

MR. STARGAZER (aside). He has made a sensation already. His noble aspect and distinguished air have produced an instantaneous impression. Mr. Grig, will you permit me? (TOM advances awkwardly.)—This is my niece, Mr. Grig,—my niece, Miss Fanny Brown; my daughter, Emma,—Mr. Thomas Grig, the favourite of the planets.

TOM. I hope I see Miss Hemmer in a conwivial state. (Aside to MR. STARGAZER.) I say, I don't know which is which.

MR. STARGAZER (aside). The young lady nearest here is your affianced bride. Say something appropriate.

TOM. Certainly; yes, of course. Let me see. Miss (crosses to her)—I—thank 'ee! (Kisses her, behind his hat. She screams.)

GALILEO (bursting from BETSY, who has been retaining him). Outrageous insolence! (Betsy runs off.)

MR. STARGAZER. Halloa, sir, halloa!

TOM. Who is this juvenile salamander, sir?

MR. STARGAZER. My little boy,—only my little boy, don't mind him. Shake hands with the gentleman, sir, instantly (to GALILEO).

TOM. A very fine boy, indeed! and he does you great credit, sir. How d' ye do, my little man? (They shake hands, GALILEO looking very wrathful, as TOM pats him on the head.) There, that's very right and proper. ''Tis dogs delight to bark and bite'; not young gentlemen, you know. There, there!

MR. STARGAZER. Now let me introduce you to that sanctum sanctorum,—that hallowed ground,— that philosophical retreat—where I, the genius loci,—

TOM. Eh?

MR. STARGAZER. The genius loci—

TOM (aside). Something to drink, perhaps. Oh, ah! yes, yes!

MR. STARGAZER. Have made all my greatest and most profound discoveries! where the telescope has almost grown to my eye with constant application; and the glass retort has been shivered to pieces from the ardour with which my experiments have been pursued. There the illustrious Mooney is, even now, pursuing those researches which will enrich us with precious metal, and make us masters of the world. Come, Mr. Grig.

TOM. By all means, sir; and luck to the illustrious Mooney, say I,—not so much on Mooney's account as for our noble selves.

MR. STARGAZER. Emma!

EMMA. Yes, papa.

MR. STARGAZER. The same day that makes your cousin Mrs. Grig, will make you and that immortal man, of whom we have just now spoken, one.

EMMA. Oh! consider, dear papa,—

MR. STARGAZER. You are unworthy of him, I know; but he,—kind, generous creature,—consents to overlook your defects, and to take you, for my sake,—devoted man!—Come, Mr. Grig!—Galileo Isaac Newton Flamstead!

GALILEO. Well? (Advancing sulkily.)

MR. STARGAZER. In name, alas! but not in nature; knowing, even by sight, no other planets than the sun and moon,—here is your weekly pocket-money,—sixpence! Take it all!

TOM. And don't spend it all at once, my man! Now, sir!

MR. STARGAZER. Now, Mr. Grig,—go first, sir, I beg!

[Exeunt TOM and MR. STARGAZER.

GALILEO. 'Come, Mr. Grig!'—'Go first, Mr. Grig!'—'Day that makes your cousin Mrs. Grig!'—I'll secretly stick a penknife into Mr. Grig, if I live to be three hours older!

FANNY (on one side of him). Oh! don't talk in that desperate way,—there's a dear, dear creature!

EMMA (on the other side). No! pray do not;—it makes my blood run cold to hear you.

GALILEO. Oh! if I was of age!—if I was only of age!—or we could go to Gretna Green, at threepence a head, including refreshments and all incidental expenses. But that could never be! Oh! if I was only of age!

FANNY. But what if you were? What could you do, then?

GALILEO. Marry you, cousin Fanny; I could marry you then lawfully, and without anybody's consent.

FANNY. You forget that, situated as we are, we could not be married, even if you were one-and-twenty;—we have no money!

EMMA. Not even enough for the fees!

GALILEO. Oh! I am sure every Christian clergyman, under such afflicting circumstances, would marry us on credit. The wedding-fees might stand over till the first christening, and then we could settle the little bill altogether. Oh! why ain't I of age!—why ain't I of age?

Enter BETSY, in haste.

BETSY. Well! I never could have believed it! There, Miss! I wouldn't have believed it, if I had dreamt it, even with a bit of bride-cake under my pillow! To dare to go and think of marrying a young lady, with five thousand pounds, to a common lamplighter!

ALL. A lamplighter?

BETSY. Yes, he's Tom Grig the lamplighter, and nothing more nor less, and old Mr. Stargazer goes and picks him out of the open street, and brings him in for Miss Fanny's husband, because he pretends to have read something about it in the stars. Stuff and nonsense! I don't believe he knows his letters in the stars, and that's the truth; or if he's got as far as words in one syllable, it's quite as much as he has.

FANNY. Was such an atrocity ever heard of? I, left with no power to marry without his consent, and he almost possessing the power to force my inclinations.

EMMA. It's actually worse than my being sacrificed to that odious and detestable Mr. Mooney.

BETSY. Come, Miss, it's not quite so bad as that neither; for Thomas Grig is a young man, and a proper young man enough too, but as to Mr. Mooney,—oh, dear! no husband is bad enough in my opinion, Miss; but he is worse than nothing,—a great deal worse.

FANNY. You seem to speak feelingly about this same Mr. Grig.

BETSY. Oh, dear no, Miss, not I. I don't mean to say but what Mr. Grig may be very well in his way, Miss; but Mr. Grig and I have never held any communication together, not even so much as how-d' ye-do. Oh, no indeed, I have been very careful, Miss, as I always am with strangers. I was acquainted with the last lamplighter, Miss, but he's going to be married, and has given up the calling, for the young woman's parents being very respectable, wished her to marry a literary man, and so he has set up as a bill-sticker. Mr. Grig only came upon this beat at five to-night, Miss.

FANNY. Which is a very sufficient reason why you don't know more of him.

BETSY. Well, Miss, perhaps it is; and I hope there's no crime in making friends in this world, if we can, Miss.

FANNY. Certainly not. So far from it, that I most heartily wish you could make something more than a friend of this Mr. Grig, and so lead him to falsify this prediction.

GALILEO. Oh! don't you think you could, Betsy?

EMMA. You could not manage at the same time to get any young friend of yours to make something more than a friend of Mr. Mooney, could you, Betsy?

GALILEO. But, seriously, don't you think you could manage to give us all a helping hand together, in some way, eh, Betsy?

FANNY. Yes, yes, that would be so delightful. I should be grateful to her for ever. Shouldn't you?

EMMA. Oh, to the very end of my life!

GALILEO. And so should I, you know, and lor'! we should make her so rich, when—when we got rich ourselves,—shouldn't we?

BOTH. Oh, that we should, of course.

BETSY. Let me see. I don't wish to have Mr. Grig to myself, you know. I don't want to be married.

ALL. No! no! no! Of course she don't.

BETSY. I haven't the least idea to put Mr. Grig off this match, you know, for anybody's sake, but you young people's. I am going quite contrairy to my own feelings, you know.

ALL. Oh, yes, yes! How kind she is!

BETSY. Well, I'll go over the matter with the young ladies in Miss Emma's room, and if we can think of anything that seems likely to help us, so much the better; and if we can't, we're none the worst. But Master Galileo mustn't come, for he is so horrid jealous of Miss Fanny that I dursn't hardly say anything before him. Why, I declare (looking off), there is my gentleman looking about him as if he had lost Mr. Stargazer, and now he turns this way. There—get out of sight. Make haste!

GALILEO. I may see 'em as far as the bottom stair, mayn't I, Betsy?

BETSY. Yes, but not a step farther on any consideration. There, get away softly, so that if he passes here, he may find me alone. (They creep gently out, GALILEO returns and peeps in.)

GALILEO. Hist, Betsy!

BETSY. Go away, sir. What have you come back for?

GALILEO (holding out a large pin). I wish you'd take an opportunity of sticking this a little way into him for patting me on the head just now.

BETSY. Nonsense, you can't afford to indulge in such expensive amusements as retaliation yet awhile. You must wait till you come into your property, sir. There.—Get you gone!

[Exit GALILEO.

Enter TOM GRIG.

TOM (aside). I never saw such a scientific file in my days. The enterprising gentleman that drowned himself to see how it felt, is nothing to him. There he is, just gone down to the bottom of a dry well in an uncommonly small bucket, to take an extra squint at the stars, they being seen best, I suppose, through the medium of a cold in the head. Halloa! Here is a young female of attractive proportions. I wonder now whether a man of noble aspect would be justified in tickling her. (He advances stealthily and tickles her under the arm.)

BETSY (startling). Eh! what! Lor', sir!

TOM. Don't be alarmed. My intentions are strictly honourable. In other words, I have no intentions whatever.

BETSY. Then you ought to be more careful, Mr. Grig. That was a liberty, sir.

TOM. I know it was. The cause of liberty, all over the world,—that's my sentiment! What is your name?

BETSY (curtseying). Betsy Martin, sir.

TOM. A name famous both in song and story. Would you have the goodness, Miss Martin, to direct me to that particular apartment wherein the illustrious Mooney is now pursuing his researches?

BETSY (aside). A little wholesome fear may not be amiss. (To him, in assumed agitation.) You are not going into that room, Mr. Grig?

TOM. Indeed, I am, and I ought to be there now, having promised to join that light of science, your master (a short six, by the bye!), outside the door.

BETSY. That dreadful and mysterious chamber! Another victim!

TOM. Victim, Miss Martin!

BETSY. Oh! the awful oath of secrecy which binds me not to disclose the perils of that gloomy, hideous room.

TOM (astonished). Miss Martin!

BETSY. Such a fine young man,—so rosy and fresh-coloured, that he should fall into the clutches of that cruel and insatiable monster! I cannot continue to witness such frightful scenes; I must give warning.

TOM. If you have anything to unfold, young woman, have the goodness to give me warning at once.

BETSY (affecting to recover herself). No, no, Mr. Grig, it's nothing,—it's ha! ha! ha!—don't mind me, don't mind me, but it certainly is very shocking;—no,—no,—I don't mean that. I mean funny,—yes. Ha! ha! ha!

TOM (aside, regarding her attentively). I suspect a trick here,—some other lover in the case who wants to come over the stars;—but it won't do. I'll tell you what, young woman (to her), if this is a cloak, you had better try it on elsewhere;—in plain English, if you have any object to gain and think to gain it by frightening me, it's all my eye and, and—yourself, Miss Martin.

BETSY. Well, then, if you will rush upon your fate,—there (pointing off)—that's the door at the end of that long passage and across the gravelled yard. The room is built away from the house on purpose.

TOM. I'll make for it at once, and the first object I inspect through that same telescope, which now and then grows to your master's eye, shall be the moon—the moon, which is the emblem of your inconstant and deceitful sex, Miss Martin.

Duet.

AIR—'The Young May-moon.'

TOM.   There comes a new moon twelve times a year.

BETSY.   And when there is none, all is dark and drear.

TOM.   In which I espy—

BETSY.   And so, too, do I—

BOTH.   A resemblance to womankind very clear.

BOTH.   There comes a new moon twelve times in a year;
                And when there is none, all is dark and drear.

TOM.   In which I espy—

BETSY.   And so do I—

BOTH.   A resemblance to womankind very clear.

Second Verse.

TOM.   She changes, she's fickle, she drives men mad.

BETSY.   She comes to bring light, and leaves them sad.

TOM.   So restless wild—

BETSY.   But so sweetly wild—

BOTH.   That no better companion could be had.

BOTH.   There comes a new moon twelve times a year;
                And when there is none, all is dark and drear.

TOM.   In which I espy—
BETSY.   And so do I—

BOTH.   A resemblance to womankind very clear.

[Exeunt.

SCENE III.—A large gloomy room; a window with a telescope directed towards the sky without, a table covered with books, instruments and apparatus, which are also scattered about in other parts of the chamber, a dim lamp, a pair of globes, etc., a skeleton in a case, and various uncouth objects displayed against the walls. Two doors in flat. MR. MOONEY discovered, with a very dirty face, busily engaged in blowing a fire, upon which is a crucible.

Enter MR. STARGAZER, with a lamp, beckoning to TOM GRIG, who enters with some unwillingness.

MR. STARGAZER. This, Mr. Grig, is the sanctum sanctorum of which I have already spoken; this is at once the laboratory and observatory.

TOM. It's not an over-lively place, is it?

MR. STARGAZER. It has an air of solemnity which well accords with the great and mysterious pursuits that are here in constant prosecution, Mr. Grig.

TOM. Ah! I should think it would suit an undertaker to the life; or perhaps I should rather say to the death. What may that cheerful object be now? (Pointing to a large phial.)

MR. STARGAZER. That contains a male infant with three heads,—we use it in astrology;—it is supposed to be a charm.

TOM. I shouldn't have supposed it myself, from his appearance. The young gentleman isn't alive, is he?

MR. STARGAZER. No, he is preserved in spirits. (MR. MOONEY sneezes.)

TOM (retreating into a corner). Halloa! What the—(MR. MOONEY looks vacantly round.) That gentleman, I suppose, is out of spirits?

MR. STARGAZER (laying his hand upon TOM'S arm and looking toward the philosopher). Hush! that is the gifted Mooney. Mark well his noble countenance,—intense thought beams from every lineament. That is the great astrologer.

TOM. He looks as if he had been having a touch at the black art. I say, why don't he say something?

MR. STARGAZER. He is in a state of abstraction; see he directs his bellows this way, and blows upon the empty air.

TOM. Perhaps he sees a strange spark in this direction and wonders how he came here. I wish he'd blow me out. (Aside.) I don't half like this.

MR. STARGAZER. You shall see me rouse him.

TOM. Don't put yourself out of the way on my account; I can make his acquaintance at any other time.

MR. STARGAZER. No time like the time present. Nothing awakens him from these fits of meditation but an electric shock. We always have a strongly charged battery on purpose. I'll give him a shock directly. (MR. STARGAZER goes up and cautiously places the end of a wire in MR. MOONEY'S hand. He then stoops down beside the table as though bringing it in contact with the battery. MR. MOONEY immediately jumps up with a loud cry and throws away the bellows.)

TOM (squaring at the philosopher). It wasn't me, you know, none of your nonsense.

MR. STARGAZER (comes hastily forward). Mr. Grig,—Mr. Grig,—not that disrespectful attitude to one of the greatest men that ever lived. This, my dear friend (to MOONEY),—is the noble stranger.

MR. MOONEY. A ha!

MR. STARGAZER. Who arrived, punctual to his time, this afternoon.

MR. MOONEY. O ho!

MR. STARGAZER. Welcome him, my friend,—give him your hand. (MR. MOONEY appears confused and raises his leg.) No—no, that's your foot. So absent, Mr. Grig, in his gigantic meditations that very often he doesn't know one from the other. Yes, that's your hand, very good, my dear friend, very good (pats MOONEY on the back as he and Tom shake hands, the latter at arm's length).

MR. STARGAZER. Have you made any more discoveries during my absence?

MR. MOONEY. Nothing particular.

MR. STARGAZER. Do you think—do you think, my dear friend, that we shall arrive at any great stage in our labours, anything at all approaching to their final consummation in the course of the night?

MR. MOONEY. I cannot take upon myself to say.

MR. STARGAZER. What are your opinions upon the subject?

MR. MOONEY. I haven't any opinions upon any subject whatsoever.

MR. STARGAZER. Wonderful man! Here's a mind, Mr. Grig.

TOM. Yes, his conversation's very improving indeed. But what's he staring so hard at me for?

MR. STARGAZER. Something occurs to him. Don't speak,—don't disturb the current of his reflections upon any account. (MR. MOONEY walks solemnly up to TOM, who retreats before him; taking off his hat turns it over and over with a thoughtful countenance and finally puts it upon his own head.)

MR. STARGAZER. Eccentric man!

TOM. I say, I hope he don't mean to keep that, because if he does, his eccentricity is unpleasant. Give him another shock and knock it off, will you?

MR. STARGAZER. Hush! hush! not a word. (MR. MOONEY, keeping his eyes fixed on TOM, slowly returns to MR. STARGAZER and whispers in his ear.)

MR. STARGAZER. Surely; by all means. I took the date of his birth, and all other information necessary for the purpose just now. (To TOM.) Mr. Mooney suggests that we should cast your nativity without delay, in order that we may communicate to you your future destiny.

MR. MOONEY. Let us retire for that purpose.

MR. STARGAZER. Certainly, wait here for a few moments, Mr. Grig: we are only going into the little laboratory and will return immediately. Now, my illustrious friend. (He takes up a lamp and leads the way to one of the doors. As MR. MOONEY follows, TOM steals behind him and regains his hat. MR. MOONEY turns round, stares, and exit through door.)

TOM. Well, that's the queerest genius I ever came across,—rather a singular person for a little smoking party. (Looks into the crucible.) This is the saucepan, I suppose, where they're boiling the philosopher's stone down to the proper consistency. I hope it's nearly done; when it's quite ready, I'll send out for sixpenn'orth of sprats, and turn 'em into gold fish for a first experiment. 'Cod! it'll be a comfortable thing though to have no end to one's riches. I'll have a country house and a park, and I'll plant a bit of it with a double row of gas-lamps a mile long, and go out with a French polished mahogany ladder, and two servants in livery behind me, to light 'em with my own hands every night. What's to be seen here? (Looks through telescope.) Nothing particular, the stopper being on at the other end. The little boy with three heads (looking towards the case). What a comfort he must have been to his parents!—Halloa! (taking up a large knife) this is a disagreeable-looking instrument,—something too large for bread and cheese, or oysters, and not of a bad shape for sticking live persons in the ribs. A very dismal place this,—I wish they'd come back. Ah!—(coming upon the skeleton) here's a ghastly object,—what does the writing say?—(reads a label upon the case) 'Skeleton of a gentleman prepared by Mr. Mooney.' I hope Mr. Mooney may not be in the habit of inviting gentlemen here, and making 'em into such preparations without their own consent. Here's a book, now. What's all this about, I wonder? The letters look as if a steam-engine had printed 'em by accident. (Turns over the leaves, spelling to himself.)

GALILEO enters softly unseen by TOM, who has his back towards him.

GALILEO (aside). Oh, you're there, are you? If I could but suffocate him, not for life, but only till I am one-and-twenty, and then revive him, what a comfort and convenience it would be! I overheard my cousin Fanny talking to Betsy about coming here. What can she want here? If she can be false,—false to me;—it seems impossible, but if she is?—well, well, we shall see. If I can reach that lumber-room unseen, Fanny Brown,—beware. (He steals toward the door on the L.—opens it, and exit cautiously into the room. As he does so, TOM turns the other way.)

TOM (closing the book). It's very pretty Greek, I think. What a time they are!

MR. STARGAZER and MOONEY enter from room.

MOONEY. Tell the noble gentleman of his irrecoverable destiny.

MR. STARGAZER (with emotion). No,—no, prepare him first.

TOM (aside). Prepare him! 'prepared by Mr. Mooney.'—This is a case of kidnapping and slaughter. (To them.) Let him attempt to prepare me at his peril!

MR. STARGAZER. Mr. Grig, why this demonstration?

TOM. Oh, don't talk to me of demonstrations;—you ain't going to demonstrate me, and so I tell you.

MR. STARGAZER. Alas! (Crossing to him.) The truth we have to communicate requires but little demonstration from our feeble lips. We have calculated upon your nativity.

MOONEY. Yes, we have, we have.

MR. STARGAZER. Tender-hearted man! (MOONEY weeps). See there, Mr. Grig, isn't that affecting?

TOM. What is he piping his boiled gooseberry eye for, sir? How should I know whether it's affecting or not?

MR. STARGAZER. For you, for you. We find that you will expire to-morrow two months, at thirty minutes—wasn't it thirty minutes, my friend?

MOONEY. Thirty-five minutes, twenty-seven seconds and five-sixths of a second. Oh! (Groans.)

MR. STARGAZER. Thirty-five minutes, twenty-seven seconds, and five-sixths of a second past nine o'clock.

MOONEY. A.M. (They both wipe their eyes.)

TOM (alarmed). Don't tell me, you've made a mistake somewhere;—I won't believe it.

MOONEY. No, it is all correct, we worked it all in the most satisfactory manner.—Oh! (Groans again.)

TOM. Satisfactory, sir! Your notions of the satisfactory are of an extraordinary nature.

MR. STARGAZER (producing a pamphlet). It is confirmed by the prophetic almanack. Here is the prediction for to-morrow two months,—'The decease of a great person may be looked for about this time.'

TOM (dropping into his chair). That's me! It's all up! inter me decently, my friends.

MR. STARGAZER (shaking his hand). Your wishes shall be attended to. We must have the marriage with my niece at once, in order that your distinguished race may be transmitted to posterity. Condole with him, my Mooney, while I compose my feelings, and settle the preliminaries of the marriage in solitude.

(Takes up lamp and exit into room R. MOONEY draws up a chair in a line with TOM, a long way off. They both sigh heavily. GALILEO opens the lumber-room door. As he does so the room door opens and BETSY steals softly in, beckoning to EMMA and FANNY who follow. He retires again abruptly.)

BETSY (aside). Now, young ladies, if you take heart only for one minute you may frighten Mr. Mooney out of being married at once.

EMMA. But if he has serious thoughts?

BETSY. Nonsense miss, he hasn't any thoughts. Your papa says to him, 'Will you marry my daughter?' and he says, 'Yes, I will'; and he would and will if you ain't bold, but bless you, he never turned it over in his mind for a minute. If you, Miss (to EMMA), pretend to hate him and love a rival, and you, Miss (to FANNY), to love him to distraction, you'll frighten him so betwixt you that he'll declare off directly, I warrant. The love will frighten him quite as much as the hate. He never saw a woman in a passion, and as to one in love, I don't believe that anybody but his mother ever kissed that grumpy old face of his in all his born days. Now, do try him, ladies. Come, we're losing time.

(She conceals herself behind the skeleton case. EMMA rushes up to TOM GRIG and embraces him, while FANNY clasps MOONEY round the neck. GALILEO appears at his door in an attitude of amazement, and MR. STARGAZER at his, after running in again with the lamp, which before he sees what is going forward he had in his hand. TOM and MOONEY in great astonishment.)

FANNY (to MOONEY). Hush! Hush!

EMMA (to GRIG).

(TOM GRIG and MOONEY get their heads sufficiently out of embrace to exchange a look of wonder.)

EMMA. Dear Mr. Grig, I know you must consider this strange, extraordinary, unaccountable conduct.

TOM. Why, ma'am, without explanation, it does appear singular.

EMMA. Yes, yes, I know it does, I know it will, but the urgency of the case must plead my excuse. Too fascinating Mr. Grig, I have seen you once and only once, but the impression of that maddening interview can never be effaced. I love you to distraction. (Falls upon his shoulder.)

TOM. You're extremely obliging, ma'am, it's a flattering sort of thing,—or it would be (aside) if I was going to live a little longer,—but you're not the one, ma'am;—it's the other lady that the stars have—

FANNY (to MOONEY). Nay, wonderful being, hear me—this is not a time for false conventional delicacy. Wrapt in your sublime visions, you have not [perceived] the silent tokens of a woman's first and all-absorbing attachment, which have been, I fear, but too perceptible in the eyes of others; but now I must speak out. I hate this odious man. You are my first and only love. Oh! speak to me.

MOONEY. I haven't anything appropriate to say, young woman. I think I had better go. (Attempting to get away.)

FANNY. Oh! no, no, no (detaining him). Give me some encouragement. Not one kind word? not one look of love?

MOONEY. I don't know how to look a look of love.—I'm, I'm frightened.

TOM. So am I! I don't understand this. I tell you, Miss, that the other lady is my destined wife. Upon my word you mustn't hug me, you'll make her jealous.

FANNY. Jealous! of you! Hear me (to MOONEY). I renounce all claim or title to the hand of that or any other man and vow to be eternally and wholly yours.

MOONEY. No, don't, you can't be mine,—nobody can be mine.—I don't want anybody—I—I—

EMMA. If you will not hear her—hear me, detested monster.—Hear me declare that sooner than be your bride, with this deep passion for another rooted in my heart,—I—

MOONEY. You need not make any declaration on the subject, young woman.

MR. STARGAZER (coming forward). She shan't,—she shan't. That's right, don't hear her. She shall marry you whether she likes it or not,—she shall marry you to-morrow morning,—and you, Miss (to FANNY), shall marry Mr. Grig if I trundle you to church in a wheelbarrow.

GALILEO (coming forward). So she shall! so she may! Let her! let her! I give her leave.

MR. STARGAZER. You give her leave, you young dog! Who the devil cares whether you give her leave or not? and what are you spinning about in that way for?

GALILEO. I'm fierce, I'm furious,—don't talk to me,—I shall do somebody a mischief;—I'll never marry anybody after this, never, never, it isn't safe. I'll live and die a bachelor!—there—a bachelor! a bachelor! (He goes up and encounters BETSY. She talks to him apart, and his wrath seems gradually to subside.)

MOONEY. The little boy, albeit of tender years, has spoken wisdom. I have been led to the contemplation of womankind. I find their love is too violent for my staid habits. I would rather not venture upon the troubled waters of matrimony.

MR. STARGAZER. You don't mean to marry my daughter? Not if I say she shall have you? (MOONEY shakes his head solemnly.) Mr. Grig, you have not changed your mind because of a little girlish folly?

TOM. To-morrow two months! I may as well get through as much gold as I can in the meantime. Why, sir, if the pot nearly boils (pointing to the crucible),—if you're pretty near the philosopher's stone,—

MR. STARGAZER. Pretty near! We're sure of it—certain; it's as good as money in the Bank. (GALILEO and BETSY, who have been listening attentively, bustle about, fanning the fire, and throwing in sundry powders from the bottles on the table, then cautiously retire to a distance.)

TOM. If that's the case, sir, I am ready to keep faith with the planets. I'll take her, sir, I'll take her.

MR. STARGAZER. Then here's her hand, Mr. Grig,—no resistance, Miss (drawing FANNY forward). It's of no use, so you may as well do it with a good grace. Take her hand, Mr. Grig. (The crucible blows up with a loud crash; they all start.)

MR. STARGAZER. What!—the labour of fifteen years destroyed in an instant!

MOONEY (stooping over the fragments). That's the only disappointment I have experienced in this process since I was first engaged in it when I was a boy. It always blows up when it's on the point of succeeding.

TOM. Is the philosopher's stone gone?

MOONEY. No.

TOM. Not gone, sir?

MOONEY. No—it never came!

MR. STARGAZER. But we'll get it, Mr. Grig. Don't be cast down, we shall discover it in less than fifteen years this time, I dare say.

TOM (relinquishing FANNY'S hand). Ah! Were the stars very positive about this union?

MR. STARGAZER. They had not a doubt about it. They said it was to be, and it must be. They were peremptory.

TOM. I am sorry for that, because they have been very civil to me in the way of showing a light now and then, and I really regret disappointing 'em. But under the peculiar circumstances of the case, it can't be.

MR. STARGAZER. Can't be, Mr. Grig! What can't be?

TOM. The marriage, sir. I forbid the banns. (Retires and sits down.)

MR. STARGAZER. Impossible! such a prediction unfulfilled! Why, the consequences would be as fatal as those of a concussion between the comet and this globe. Can't be! it must be, shall be.

BETSY (coming forward, followed by GALILEO). If you please, sir, may I say a word?

MR. STARGAZER. What have you got to say?—speak, woman!

BETSY. Why, sir, I don't think Mr. Grig is the right man.

MR. STARGAZER. What!

BETSY. Don't you recollect, sir, that just as the house-clock struck the first stroke of five, you gave Mr. Galileo a thump on the head with the butt end of your telescope, and told him to get out of the way?

MR. STARGAZER. Well, if I did, what of that?

BETSY. Why, then, sir, I say, and I would say it if I was to be killed for it, that he's the young gentleman that ought to marry Miss Fanny, and that the stars never meant anything else.

MR. STARGAZER. He! Why, he's a little boy.

GALILEO. I ain't. I'm one-and-twenty next Lady-day.

MR. STARGAZER. Eh! Eighteen hundred and—why, so he is, I declare. He's quite a stranger to me, certainly. I never thought about his age since he was fourteen, and I remember that birthday, because he'd a new suit of clothes then. But the noble family—

BETSY. Lor', sir! ain't it being of noble family to be the son of such a clever man as you?

MR. STARGAZER. That's true. And my mother's father would have been Lord Mayor, only he died of turtle the year before.

BETSY. Oh, it's quite clear.

MR. STARGAZER. The only question is about the time, because the church struck afterwards. But I should think the stars, taking so much interest in my house, would most likely go by the house-clock,—eh! Mooney?

MOONEY. Decidedly,—yes.

MR. STARGAZER. Then you may have her, my son. Her father was a great astronomer; so I hope that, though you are a blockhead, your children may be scientific. There! (Joins their hands.)

EMMA. Am I free to marry who I like, papa?

MR. STARGAZER. Won't you, Mooney? Won't you?

MOONEY. If anybody asks me to again I'll run away, and never come back any more.

MR. STARGAZER. Then we must drop the subject. Yes, your choice is now unfettered.
EMMA. Thank you, dear papa. Then I'll look about for somebody who will suit me without the delay of an instant longer than is absolutely necessary.

MR. STARGAZER. How very dutiful!

FANNY. And, as my being here just now with Emma was a little trick of Betsy's, I hope you'll forgive her, uncle.

EMMA / GALILEO Oh, yes, do.

FANNY. And even reward her, uncle, for being instrumental in fulfilling the prediction.

EMMA / GALILEO   Oh, yes; do reward her—do.

FANNY. Perhaps you could find a husband for her, uncle, you know. Don't you understand?

BETSY. Pray don't mention it, Miss. I told you at first, Miss, that I had not the least wish or inclination to have Mr. Grig to myself. I couldn't abear that Mr. Grig should think I wanted him to marry me; oh no, Miss, not on any account.

MR. STARGAZER. Oh, that's pretty intelligible. Here, Mr. Grig. (They fall back from his chair.) Have you any objection to take this young woman for better, for worse?

BETSY. Lor', sir! how ondelicate!

MR. STARGAZER. I'll add a portion of ten pounds for your loss of time here to-night. What do you say, Mr. Grig?

TOM. It don't much matter. I ain't long for this world. Eight weeks of marriage might reconcile me to my fate. I should go off, I think, more resigned and peaceful. Yes, I'll take her, as a reparation. Come to my arms! (He embraces her with a dismal face.)

MR. STARGAZER (taking a paper from his pocket). Egad! that reminds me of what I came back to say, which all this bustle drove out of my head. There's a figure wrong in the nativity (handing the paper to MOONEY). He'll live to a green old age.

TOM (looking up). Eh! What?

MOONEY. So he will. Eighty-two years and twelve days will be the lowest.

TOM (disengaging himself). Eh! here! (calling off). Hallo, you, sir! bring in that ladder and lantern.

A SERVANT enters in great haste, and hands them to TOM.

SERVANT. There's such a row in the street,—none of the gas-lamps lit, and all the people calling for the lamplighter. Such a row!

TOM (rubbing his hands with great glee). Is there, my fine fellow? Then I'll go and light 'em. And as, under existing circumstances, and with the prospect of a green old age before me, I'd rather not be married, Miss Martin, I beg to assure the ratepayers present that in future I shall pay the strictest attention to my professional duties, and do my best for the contractor; and that I shall be found upon my beat as long as they condescend to patronize the Lamplighter. (Runs off. MISS MARTIN faints in the arms of MOONEY.)

CURTAIN

Charles Dickens - A Short Biography

Charles Dickens (1812-1870) is regarded by many readers and literary critics to be THE major English novelist of the Victorian Age. He is remembered today as the author of a series of weighty novels which have been translated into many languages and promoted to the rank of World Classics. The latter include, but are not limited to, *The Adventures of Oliver Twist*, *A Tale of Two Cities*, *David Copperfield*, *A Christmas Carol*, *Hard Times*, *Great Expectations* and *The Old Curiosity Shop*.

Birth and Childhood's Hardships

By and large, Charles Dickens's life story is one of somebody who is born and raised in dire straits to become one of the greatest men who have marked human history and thought. It is a perfect example of how the plight of the deprived and the destitute could transform into a precious incentive that pushes them to challenge their circumstances and to unexpectedly excel and shine.

Charles Dickens was born in Portsmouth on February 7th, 1812. His father John Dickens worked as a simple accounting clerk at the Naval Pay Office and the family's pecuniary situation was almost always uneven. When Charles was only two years, the family had to move to London, then later to Chatham. For financial reasons, Charles did not have adequate education. He rather had to leave school at a very young age to work at a polishing and blacking factory. To add insult to injury, Charles's father was imprisoned in 1824 after failing to pay a 40-pound debt.

Charles's experience at the factory played a tremendous role in building the novelist's personality and in deepening his concerns about working children and about the working class in general. Dickens's precocious maturity and the serious responsibilities that he had as a little child left a clear impression on many of his young characters, such as Oliver Twist, David Copperfield and Pip in *Great Expectations*. The hardships that Charles Dickens personally went through made him much interested in defending the poor, in fighting social injustice through exposing its blatant manifestations and in accentuating the importance of having decent work conditions.

Between 1824 and 1827, Dickens's father, who eventually managed to pay his debts, offered Charles the opportunity to attend a private school in North London, the Wellington House Academy. The experience surely enriched the young man's knowledge of the rules of writing and rhetoric and whetted his appetite for 18th-century novels and for the picaresque novels that adorned his father's library. However, during this period, Charles still had to experience another disappointment when his mother refused to spare him the strenuous job at the blacking factory even after the relative improvement of the family's financial situation. The mother's decision had a great psychological impact on young Charles and even influenced his vision of gender roles as he thought that the mother should not be the decision-maker in the family.

Early Publications

Young Charles Dickens occupied numerous jobs and worked hard to learn shorthand. This long and diversified professional experience had a patent impact on his different writings. Indeed, after the blacking factory experience, Dickens first worked as a clerk for attorneys, which allowed him to learn about the legal system and its principles, to become a free-lance reporter for Doctor's Commons Courts in 1829. Later, he even wrote reports for the House of Commons before starting to work for newspapers, magazines and journals.

It was in 1833 that Dickens started writing short stories for a number of literary magazines and journals such as *The Monthly Magazine*. A collection of these texts was later pseudonymously published under the title *Sketches by Boz*. Thanks to Dickens's humor and exceptional writing style, the latter publication was relatively successful, but not as successful as *The Pickwick Papers* whose serial publication sold thousands of copies and raised Dickens to considerable fame. In 1836, he started writing short texts to be published with the humorous illustrations of the famous artist Robert Seymour. These first successes encouraged Dickens to carry on publishing other stories in the form of series. Dickens's next creation was *Oliver Twist* which was published between 1837 and 1839.

It is noteworthy that most of Dickens's novels were published in the form of monthly and weekly chapters which, according to critics and biographers, allowed him to evaluate and adjust his characterizations and plots to meet the expectations of his readership. It was also during this period that Dickens started his long career as a literary magazine editor.

Loves and Marriage

Charles Dickens got married on April 2nd, 1836 to Catherine Thomson Hogarth after one year of engagement. They settled at the famous Furnival's Inn in Holborn, London, before they moved to their home in Bloomsbury. The house was transformed into the Charles Dickens Museum in 1925. Charles and Catherine, who lived there with the first three of their ten children, were joined by Charles's brother Frederick and Catherine's sister Mary. The latter was reported to have had a very special place in Charles's heart. After dying in his own arms in 1837 following a sudden illness, she became a source of inspiration for some of his female characters. After three years of marriage, Dickens's success and rising income made him leave the house for larger and more luxurious estates.

Catherine Hogarth was not Dickens's only love, however. Indeed, biographers report that Dickens's relation with his wife was sandwiched by two other romantic affairs. First, there was Maria Beadnell, a banker's daughter, with whom Dickens fell in love when he was only eighteen years old. The relationship ended three years later when Maria's parents apparently intervened. The other love story that Dickens went through started in 1857 and pushed him to divorce Catherine the following year. It was when Dickens was having a group of young actresses for the staging of his play *The Frozen Deep* that he fell in love with the actress Ellen Ternan who was 27 years younger than him.

Major Achievements

Charles's first success with *The Pickwick Papers* and *Oliver Twist* only pushed him to devote more time and energy to his writing and editorial activities. After publishing *Nicholas Nickleby* between 1838 and 1839, he started a new project in 1840 that he entitled *Master Humphrey's Clock*. The latter is a collection of stories that share the same frame and have recurring characters. It was among this collection that the two major works *The Old Curiosity Shop* and *Barnaby Rudge* were serially published.

After visiting the United States of America in 1842, Dickens developed a rather negative view of the New World which was mainly depicted in his travelogue *American Notes for General Circulation* and also in his picaresque novel *Martin Chuzzlewit*. The latter included very harsh satire of the republic and strongly denounced its institution of slavery. However, the fury that Dickens caused among some American circles was soon quietened with the publication of *A Christmas Carol* in 1843. The book, which is considered by many as the novelist's finest opus, was celebrated both in England and America.

Two other Christmas books followed respectively in 1834 and 1845. They are *The Chimes* and *The Cricket on the Hearth*. During this period, Dickens also published a new travelogue that he entitled *Pictures from Italy* following his stay in the Mediterranean country. Another Christmas story entitled *The Haunted Man* was published in 1848, which was preceded by *Dombey and Son* (1847) and *The Battle of Life* (1847) and followed by David Copperfield (1849-1850), *Bleak House* (1852-1853) and *Hard Times* (1854).

It was in 1853 that Dickens started organizing public performances in which he presented his literary works. By this time, he also started to collaborate with Wilkie Collins on a number of short stories and plays. *Little Dorrit* started as a monthly serial in 1855 to be finished in 1857. Later, two of Dickens's most valuable works were published: *A Tale of Two Cities* (1859) and *Great Expectations* (1861). They were both published in the weekly periodical, *All the Year Round*, which he founded and edited himself.

Apart from his writings, Dickens's main profitable activity was the public reading of his novels. Along with the money he earned thanks to his successful publications, public readings allowed Dickens to buy his dream house (Gad's Hill Place, Kent), to offer financial help to his parents and brothers and to engage in charitable activities.

Twilight and Death

During the 1860s, Dickens carried on organizing more reading tours. In addition to the many events he had in England, he visited France, the United States, Scotland and Ireland on many an occasion. In 1864, he started his last complete novel, *Our Mutual Friend*. However, by 1865, his health started to waver. This was mainly because of the physical and intellectual exhaustion to which he subjected himself. Furthermore, Dickens was psychologically traumatized in 1865 following a train crash. He was with his beloved Ellen Ternan on their way back from Paris when their train derailed to cause a big number of casualties. Although Dickens was able to collect his courage and managed to help the wounded and comfort them, the picture of the disaster affected him greatly and could never be erased from his mind.

For health reasons, Dickens cancelled many of his programmed readings between 1868 and 1870. On April 22nd, 1869, he had a stroke. The latter was followed by a second stroke on June 8th, 1870, while he was working on his novel *The Mystery of Edwin Drood* which would remain unfinished. The next day, he passed away. Charles Dickens today rests in The Poets' Corner of Westminster Abbey.